Shakespeare Mini-Books

**8 Reproducible Comic Book–Style Retellings of Favorite Plays
That Will Wow Kids With the Works & Words of Shakespeare**

by Jeannette Sanderson

NEW YORK • TORONTO • LONDON • AUCKLAND • SYDNEY
MEXICO CITY • NEW DELHI • HONG KONG • BUENOS AIRES

SCHOLASTIC
Teaching
Resources

Dedication

For all teachers who inspire a love of language in their students

Acknowledgments

I would like to thank my editor, Virginia Dooley, for giving me this assignment, and with it the chance to read Shakespeare all over again.

Cover design by Maria Lilja
Interior design by Russell Bart
Illustrations by Miracle Studios

ISBN 0-439-36601-1
Copyright © 2003 by Jeannette Sanderson
All rights reserved.
Printed in the U.S.A.

2 3 4 5 6 7 8 9 10   40   09 08 07 06 05 04 03

Contents

Mini-Books:

About This Book

This collection of eight mini-books will introduce students to the works of William Shakespeare. These plays, adapted and written in comic-book form, should appeal to all students. The narrative of each book is written in contemporary English, with an occasional line from Shakespeare, to make the stories fairly easy to follow. Students will not miss out on Shakespeare's magnificent use of language, however, as nearly all of the words the characters speak in the mini-books—their dialogue and thought bubbles—are Shakespeare's own.

You'll find background information on each Shakespeare play mini-book on pages 9–16, as well as easy classroom activities to help supplement your lessons. There is also a "Bard Card" for each play. These cards provide a brief plot summary, a list of the main characters, and a glossary of difficult or unfamiliar words. You may wish to copy these cards and share them with your students to help them with their reading.

A brief overview of Shakespeare's life and works, along with a list of books for further reading, starts on page 5.

How to Make the Mini-Books

1. Carefully tear along the perforation to remove the mini-book pages you want to use. Make double-sided photocopies of the mini-book pages.

*NOTE: If your photocopy machine does not have a double-sided function, follow these directions:

• First, make copies of the first full page of the mini-book (pages 1 and 3).

• Place the copies in the paper tray with the blank side facing up.

• Next, make a copy of the second full page of the mini-book (pages 2 and 4) so that the page copies directly behind mini-book pages 1 and 3.

• Make a test copy to be sure the pages are aligned correctly and that mini-book page 2 appears directly behind mini-book page 1.

• Repeat these steps with the rest of the mini-book pages.

2. Cut the double-sided mini-book pages along the dashed line.

3. Place the pages in numerical order, and then staple them along the mini-book's spine.

About Shakespeare

William Shakespeare is considered the greatest playwright who ever lived. During his lifetime, Shakespeare wrote 37 plays as well as a number of poems. While that would be impressive during any age, what is most amazing about Shakespeare is that he wrote 400 years ago, and his works are as popular today as they were when they were written. In the words of Shakespeare's fellow dramatist and admirer Ben Johnson, "He was not of an age, but for all time!"

Shakespeare's Life

Very little is known for certain about Shakespeare's life. What is known is based primarily on his works, as well as church and legal documents that have survived from Elizabethan times. The church and legal documents sketch out details of the early part of his life.

William Shakespeare was born in Stratford-upon-Avon, England, most likely on April 23, 1564 (church records from Holy Trinity Church show that he was baptized on April 26), the third of eight children born to John Shakespeare and Mary Arden. John was a successful merchant, and his son William probably went to the well-regarded free grammar school in Stratford. Though his work demonstrates a solid education in the

classics, Shakespeare did not attend university.

Shakespeare married Anne Hathaway on November 28, 1582. They had three children: Susanna, born May 26, 1583, and Hamnet and Judith, born February 2, 1585. (Hamnet died on August 11, 1596.)

No records exist of Shakespeare's life for the seven years after the birth of his twins. Then in 1592, Shakespeare appeared in London. In a pamphlet, playwright Robert Green warned other university-educated playwrights of an actor who also presumed to be a playwright. This warning read: "There is an upstart crow, beautified with our feathers, that with his tiger's heart wrapped in a player's hide supposes he is as well able to bombast out a blank verse as the best of you, and being an absolute Johannes-factotum [i.e., Jack of all trades],

is in his own conceit the only Shake-scene in the country." Scholars believe that Shakespeare must have been in London for at least several years prior to this diatribe: He would have needed that much time to establish himself well enough to earn Green's envy.

Within two years after Green published his hostile comments, Shakespeare was acting and writing for the Lord Chamberlain's Men (which became the King's Men after James I became ruler in 1603). This troupe, patronized by royalty and commoners alike, first performed at "The Theatre" on the outskirts of London. In 1599, the Lord Chamberlain's Men built the Globe Theatre across the Thames River in Bankside, and performed there.

Shakespeare stayed with the King's Men until he retired to Stratford-upon-Avon, about 1611. He died in the town where he was born, allegedly on his 52nd birthday. His tombstone at Holy Trinity Church bears this epitaph, which he is said to have written:

Good friend for Jesus' sake forbear,
To dig the dust enclosed here:
Blest be the man that spares these stones,
And curst be he that moves my bones.

These words proved powerful enough to keep his bones from being disturbed in a crowded burial ground, where it was common to remove old bones to make way for new.

Shakespeare's Works

As with his life, there is very little concrete evidence as to the chronology of Shakespeare's works. Scholars have had to rely on topic and content to make educated guesses about when his plays and poems were written.

Shakespeare's plays are generally divided into three main categories: histories, comedies, and tragedies. Shakespeare's early history plays had less characterization than his later ones. His early comedies were farcical while his latest were dark enough to sometimes be called tragicomedies. His tragedies grew in depth and became increasingly symbolic.

While 18 of Shakespeare's plays appeared in print during his lifetime, the main source of Shakespeare's works is the 1623 Folio volume of *Mr. William Shakespeare's Comedies, Histories, & Tragedies*. This first collected edition of Shakespeare included 36 plays. The Folio has proven itself an invaluable resource, even though it was incomplete—it leaves out two plays believed to be written, at least in large part, by Shakespeare: *Pericles, Prince of Tyre* and *The Two Noble Kinsmen*, and also omits Shakespeare's nondramatic

poems, except his sonnets.

Although best known as a playwright, Shakespeare was also a remarkable poet. His Sonnets, which are numbered 1 to 152, are considered his major poetic achievement.

Below is a list of Shakespeare's works, and the approximate dates he is believed to have composed them.

Plays

1588–94	*The Comedy of Errors*
1588–94	*Love's Labor's Lost*
1589–92	*Henry VI, Part I*
1589–92	*Henry VI, Part II*
1589–91	*Henry VI, Part III*
1589–93	*Richard III*
1589–94	*Titus Andronicus*
1592–94	*The Two Gentlemen of Verona*
1593–94	*The Taming of the Shrew*
1594–96	*The Merchant of Venice*
1594–96	*Romeo and Juliet*
1595	*Richard II*
1595–96	*A Midsummer Night's Dream*
1596–97	*King John*
1596–97	*Henry IV, Part I*
1597	*The Merry Wives of Windsor*
1597–98	*Henry IV, Part II*
1598–99	*Much Ado About Nothing*
1598–99	*Henry V*
1599	*Julius Caesar*
1599–1600	*As You Like It*
1599–1600	*Twelfth Night*
1600–01	*Hamlet*
1601–02	*Troilus and Cressida*
1602–04	*All's Well That Ends Well*
1603–04	*Othello*
1604	*Measure for Measure*
1605–06	*King Lear*
1605–06	*Macbeth*
1605–08	*Timon of Athens*
1606–07	*Antony and Cleopatra*
1607–08	*Coriolanus*
1607–08	*Pericles*
1609–10	*Cymbeline*
1610–11	*The Winter's Tale*
1611	*The Tempest*
1612–13	*Henry VIII*
1613	*The Two Noble Kinsmen*

Poems

1592–93	*Venus and Adonis*
1593–94	*The Rape of Lucrece*
1593–1600	*Sonnets*
1600–1601	*The Phoenix and the Turtle*

Resources

Books

Aagesen, Colleen, and Margie Blumberg. *Shakespeare for Kids: His Life and Times: 21 Activities.* Chicago: Chicago Review Press, 1999.

Egan, Lorraine Hopping. *Teaching Shakespeare—Yes You Can!* New York: Scholastic Professional Books, 1998.

Greenblatt, Stephen, Walter Cohen, Jean E. Howard, Katherine Eisaman Maus, editors. *The Norton Shakespeare: Based on the Oxford Edition.* New York: W.W. Norton & Company, Inc., 1997.

Miller, Carol Rawlings. *Irresistible Shakespeare.* New York: Scholastic Professional Books, 2001.

Internet Sites

THE COMPLETE WORKS OF WILLIAM SHAKESPEARE
http://the-tech.mit.edu/Shakespeare
This site contains the Web's first edition of the complete works of William Shakespeare.

MR. WILLIAM SHAKESPEARE AND THE INTERNET
http://shakespeare.palomar.edu
This site, which attempts to be a complete annotated guide to scholarly Shakespeare resources on the Internet, has some wonderful links.

SHAKESPEARE'S GLOBE RESEARCH DATABASE
http://www.rdg.ac.uk/globe
This site, sponsored by the University of Reading (United Kingdom), is dedicated to providing background information on Shakespearean performances in original conditions, i.e., contemporary London and its playhouses, especially Shakespeare's Globe Theatre.

SHAKESPEARE RESOURCE CENTER
http://www.bardweb.net
Among other things, this site offers background information on Shakespeare, his works, and the Globe Theatre, as well as play synopses. It also includes useful links to other Shakespeare Web sites.

SHAKESPEARE.COM
http://www.shakespeare.com
This site is devoted to the popular enjoyment of Shakespeare's works.

TEACHING SHAKESPEARE
http://www.folger.edu/education/teaching.htm
This site contains teacher-created lesson plans from the Folger Shakespeare Library, the world's most significant repository of Shakespearean material.

Hamlet

Hamlet, written around 1600 and first published in 1603, is probably Shakespeare's most famous play, and certainly one of his most widely discussed. Experts consider this play an enigma—it raises far more questions than it answers.

The Tragedy of Hamlet, *Prince of Denmark* was the first of Shakespeare's great tragedies. It was also the first play that introduced—in Shakespeare's writing and in Western drama—a new kind of literary subjectivity, in which the audience gets to know what is happening inside a character's head. In fact, Hamlet is so contemplative that some critics have cited this thinking in place of action as one of his character flaws.

Though the play deals with many Renaissance ideas—honor, revenge, justice, political order, stoicism, and friendship—it is actually based on an ancient story that was passed along orally until Saxo Grammaticus wrote it in the 12th century in his *Historica Danica*. Shakespeare modernized the story and made the play his own by his use of language. He introduced more than 600 words in *Hamlet*; many of them do not appear in any other English text.

Activity: Invite students to write and perform a brief skit in which a group of actors performs the scene where the king is murdered by his brother. Students may include Hamlet, Queen Gertrude, and King Claudius in the audience, and incorporate their reactions to the mini-play into the skit.

BARD CARD | ## Hamlet

Plot Summary: In this tragedy, Prince Hamlet learns that his uncle murdered his father and married his mother to become king. The events take place in Elsinore, Denmark, around 1200.

Main Characters

Hamlet: Prince of Denmark
King Claudius: Hamlet's uncle (his late father's brother), his mother's new husband
Queen Gertrude: Hamlet's mother, new wife of King Claudius
Polonius: a lord
Laertes: Polonius's son
Ophelia: Hamlet's beloved, Polonius's daughter
Horatio: Hamlet's friend
Rosencrantz and Guildenstern: Hamlet's former friends

Glossary

afflicts: troubles
aught: anything
ay: yes
battlements: a wall with open spaces that is used for defense
beckons: calls
beseech: beg
bier: a coffin and its stand
bore: carried
envenom'd: poisoned
fain: willing
glean: find out
issue: outcome
lament: cry of grief

perchance: maybe
stalk: to walk stiffly
unprevailing: uncommon
woe: grief, sadness

Julius Caesar

Julius Caesar, probably written around 1599, was the first of Shakespeare's Roman plays, and his earliest tragedy.

The play explores the conflict between principle and pragmatism. Shakespeare shows that brutal pragmatism may sometimes serve society better than noble idealism. Despite Brutus's best intentions, Rome was a more stable, just, and free place when Caesar was alive.

Shakespeare strongly believed in the divine quality of kingship and the stability it provided. Around the time *Julius Caesar* was written, Queen Elizabeth I was nearing the end of her rule and had yet to name an heir. Shakespeare was anticipating the chaos that could follow if sovereign power was not transferred in traditional, accepted ways.

Shakespeare based this play on Thomas North's 1579 English translation of *Plutarch's Lives of the Noble Grecians and Romans*. In his play, Shakespeare condensed into three days events that in actuality took place over a period of three years.

Activity: Divide the class into pairs. Assign each pair a controversial topic (e.g., year-round school, school uniforms), and have each student in the pair choose a side, pro or con. Have students write and present short speeches, in pairs, to the class. Discuss with the class how each speech swayed their thinking, and which parts of each speech moved them. Ask how this compares to what happened at Caesar's funeral after Brutus and Antony each spoke.

BARD CARD | ## Julius Caesar

Plot Summary: This tragedy is Shakespeare's version of the murder of the ancient Roman ruler Julius Caesar (100–44 B.C.) and the eventual defeat of the conspirators who killed him.

Main Characters
Julius Caesar: dictator of Rome
Mark Antony: Caesar's friend
Marcus Brutus: a conspirator against Caesar
Caius Cassius: a conspirator against Caesar
Octavius Caesar: Caesar's grandnephew
Calpurnia: Caesar's wife

Glossary
Et tu, Brute: You too, Brutus
Forum: the center and public meeting place of the city
ides of March: March 15th
ingrafted: deep
issue: deed
legions: large military forces
oration: a formal speech
redress: correct
soothsayer: prophet
Tarquin: an earlier Roman ruler who was overthrown
whelped: gave birth

King Lear

King Lear, probably written around 1605–1606, is one of Shakespeare's tragic masterpieces, though, not a completely original one. The earliest account of the tale is in Geoffrey of Monmouth's 12th-century *Historia Regum Brittaniae*. Shakespeare probably used Raphael Holinshed's 1587 version in *The Chronicles of England, Scotlande, and Irelande*.

Shakespeare also drew from current events in writing this play. In 1603, the two eldest daughters of Sir Brian Annesley sued to have their father declared legally insane so they could take over his estate. His youngest daughter, Cordell, protested on his behalf. Whatever his sources, Shakespeare made the story immeasurably moving and all his own.

King Lear is mostly a domestic play, dealing with a family's fears and tensions. In Shakespeare's time, the father held sovereignty over his family just as a king held sovereignty over his land. The play also explores other themes, including power and powerlessness, appearance and reality, wisdom and folly, youth and age, and sight and blindness (both physical and intellectual).

Activity: Ask each student to write a one-page essay, telling what they think a child owes his or her parents, and how they think Shakespeare's three daughters measured up to what they believe are a child's filial duties. Invite students to share their essays and discuss the question: What does a child owe his or her parents?

BARD CARD | ## King Lear

Plot Summary: *King Lear*, which takes place in Britain in the first century B.C., is the story of an old king whose foolish pride causes him to lose his kingdom, the only daughter who loves him, and his life.

Main Characters
King Lear: old king of Britain
Goneril: Lear's first daughter
Regan: Lear's second daughter
Cordelia: Lear's youngest and once-favorite daughter
Earl of Kent: King Lear's friend
Earl of Gloucester: Lear's honest subject
Duke of Albany: Goneril's honest husband
Duke of Cornwall: Regan's husband
Edgar: Earl of Gloucester's legitimate son
Edmund: Earl of Gloucester's traitorous illegitimate son

Glossary
apprehension: arrest
banish'd: exiled; required to leave the country
dowry: the money, goods, or estate that a woman brings to her husband in marriage
hovel: hut
overture: introduction
pawn: a person that can be used to further the purposes of another person
procure: bring about

rack: an instrument of torture on which a body is stretched
raiment: clothing
steward: supervisor of servants
stocks: a wooden frame with holes in which the feet and hands can be locked as punishment
tempest: a violent storm
vouchsafe: to grant or furnish
writ: a written order

Macbeth

Macbeth is the shortest of Shakespeare's great tragedies. It also differs from the others in that it has no subplot.

While there is no definitive date for the first publication or performance of *Macbeth*, scholars generally date this play to the year 1606. Shakespeare appears to have written this play to please and honor the Scottish King James, who ascended the throne after Queen Elizabeth's death in 1603. Within months of becoming king, Shakespeare's company, the Lord Chamberlain's Men, was formally declared the King's Men. Shakespeare showed his and the company's gratitude by writing *Macbeth*, in which Banquo, one of the king's ancestors, is a hero.

Shakespeare loosely based his play on a story found in Raphael Holinshed's *The Chronicles of England, Scotlande, and Irelande.* One of the great liberties he took in rewriting this history included making Banquo a hero, instead of a conspirator in the murder of the king that Holinshed's *Chronicles* tells us he was.

Activity: Ask students to imagine the letter that *Macbeth* wrote to his wife after his encounter with the three witches. Then have them write a letter they think he might have sent.

BARD CARD | Macbeth

Plot Summary: *Macbeth* is the story of a Scottish noble who murders his king to gain the throne, and the consequences of his actions. The story takes place in Scotland in the 11th century.

Main Characters
Macbeth: a Scottish thane
Lady Macbeth: his wife
Duncan: King of Scotland
Banquo: a Scottish chieftain
Malcolm: King Duncan's son
Macduff: a Scottish thane
Witches

Glossary
bane: destruction
bed chamber: bedroom
bough: a branch of a tree
chamber: bedroom
harness: armor
heath: an area of wasteland
imperial: relating to an empire or emperor
kinsman: relative
prologues: introductory events
prophesying: making predictions

Scone: ancient royal city where Scottish kings were crowned
thane: a Scottish feudal lord
usurper: one who wrongfully seizes power
vanquish'd: overcome in battle
wrack: ruin, destruction

A Midsummer Night's Dream

Scholars place Shakespeare's writing of this comedy—one of his most popular works—between 1595 and 1596. There is some debate as to whether or not Shakespeare wrote it to be performed at an aristocratic wedding, just as the tradesmen's play in *A Midsummer Night's Dream* was written for the duke's wedding. Plays were often part of the entertainment at upper-class weddings during Elizabethan times.

Most of the play takes place in the fairy-infested dream world of the woods outside Athens. There is no single literary source for the dream world Shakespeare created in this play. But Elizabethans believed in fairies, so this world would have been very believable to them. Shakespeare explores a number of themes, including the capriciousness and changeability of love.

The title of the play refers to Midsummer Eve, celebrated on June 23, the day of the summer solstice. This evening was celebrated with festivities, temporary madness, and stories of fairy spells. Tradition also held that on Midsummer Eve you would dream of the person you were going to marry.

Activity: Have each student design a poster for *A Midsummer Night's Dream*. Compare and discuss how each student chose to represent the play. You might also include the illustration used on the cover of the mini-book in your discussion.

BARD CARD | A Midsummer Night's Dream

Plot Summary: This comedy, in which men and women—with the help of fairies—fall in and out of love, takes place in ancient Greece, in and around Athens.

Main Characters

Theseus: Duke of Athens
Hippolyta: Queen of the Amazons, Theseus's fiancée
Egeus: father of Hermia
Hermia: a maiden in love with Lysander
Helena: a maiden in love with Demetrius
Lysander: a young man in love with Hermia
Demetrius: a young man also in love with Hermia
Oberon: king of the fairies
Titania: queen of the fairies
Robin Goodfellow: fairy page to Oberon; also known as Puck
Nick Bottom: a carpenter, would-be actor, and temporary love object of the queen

Glossary

amity: friendship
changeling: a child secretly changed for another in infancy
churl: a rude, ill-bred person
derision: the use of scorn to show contempt
disdainful: full of scorn
enamour'd: charmed
enthralled: charmed
eyne: eyes
henchman: page; male attendant

lamenting: expressing sorrow
mock: to ridicule; to make fun of
nymphs: minor divinities of nature in classical mythology, represented by beautiful maidens
page: a boy attendant
puck: a mischievous sprite
rebuke: express strong disapproval
render: give up, yield
revels: celebrations
woo'd: courted

Much Ado About Nothing

Much Ado About Nothing, written in 1598 and first published in 1600, is a romantic comedy that takes place in aristocratic circles in 13th-century Italy. It offers plenty of humor, but a touch of sadness as well.

The play weaves together the story of two sets of lovers: Beatrice and Benedick, who are brought together by the workings of their friends and relatives; and Hero and Claudio, who are nearly destroyed by a person's deceit and trickery.

One of the main themes of this play is perception. In both love stories, at least one member of the couple overhears something that alters his or her feelings for the other. Elizabethan audiences would have been tipped off to the plot by its title—"nothing" was pronounced "noting" back then. The characters note rather than see, and as a result are easily induced to fall in or out of love. The play also deals with the themes of honor and shame, as well as loyalty—very important ideas in Elizabethan times.

Activity: Ask students to imagine they are Beatrice or Benedick, and write a sonnet to the other after they have overheard of the other's supposed love for them. (An English sonnet is a 14-line poem with the rhyme scheme *abab cdcd efef gg*, and the rhythm in iambic pentameter, *da DA da DA da DA da DA*, with the capitalized "DA" representing the stressed syllables.) Discuss with students what the sonnets might have been like before each believed the other loved them. Some students might want to write "before" and "after" sonnets.

BARD CARD Much Ado About Nothing

Plot Summary: *Much Ado About Nothing* is the story of two pairs of lovers, one brought together by meddling, and the other, almost destroyed by it. This comedy takes place in 13th-century Italy.

Main Characters
Don Pedro: Prince of Arragon
Leonato: Governor of Messina
Benedick: a young lord
Claudio: a young lord
Hero: Leonato's daughter
Beatrice: Leonato's niece
Don John: Don Pedro's evil half-brother

Glossary
arrant: extreme
confirmed: fixed in a habit and unlikely to change
cunning: clever
defiled: dishonored
disdain: to look down on something
ducats: gold coins
knave: a tricky, deceitful person
meet: fit
prolong'd: lengthened in time

reconciled: had resolved their differences
requite: repay
ruffian: a brutal person; a bully
wanton: a person who is indecent or morally offensive
wooed: courted
yield: give up

Romeo and Juliet

Romeo and Juliet, written around 1594, is one of Shakespeare's most popular plays and is considered one of the greatest love stories ever written.

Originally called *The Most Excellent and Lamentable Tragedy of Romeo and Juliet*, the play is a tragedy of fate rather than of flaws. Romeo's family, the Montagues, has had a long and bitter rivalry with Juliet's family, the Capulets. Romeo and Juliet fell in love before they knew each other's names.

This story of ill-fated love had been told many times in Italian, French, and English. Shakespeare's primary source was Arthur Brooke's 1562 poem, *Tragical History of Romeus and Juliet*. But Shakespeare's brilliant use of language makes his version the one we remember. Romeo and Juliet speak their devotion in poetry—the conversation at their first meeting is a shared sonnet—and prose. Shakespeare plays with language throughout, using paradoxes, oxymorons, double entendres, rhyming tricks, and puns.

Activity: Ask each student to choose a major event in the story and write a diary entry about it from Romeo or Juliet's point of view. For example, Juliet might write after she and Romeo profess their love to each other, when she learns that Romeo has killed Tybalt and is banished, or when her parents order her to marry Paris. Romeo might write after he and Juliet profess their love to each other, after he kills Tybalt, or when he hears that Juliet is dead.

BARD CARD | Romeo and Juliet

Plot Summary: *Romeo and Juliet* is the story of the brief courtship and early deaths of two star-crossed lovers from bitterly feuding Italian families, the Montagues and the Capulets. This tragedy takes place in the 1400s in Verona, Italy.

Main Characters

Romeo: son of Montague
Juliet: daughter of Capulet
Mercutio: Romeo's friend
Benvolio: Romeo's friend
Tybalt: Lady Capulet's nephew, enemy of Romeo
Nurse: Juliet's attendant
Friar Laurence
Prince of Verona

Glossary

cordial: a kind of liquor
disparagement: to speak of as unimportant
doff: to get rid of
dram: a small portion of something to drink
foe: enemy
gall: bitterness
hence: from this place
hie: hasten; go quickly
sheath: a case for a blade
woe: deep sorrow

The Tempest

The Tempest, written around 1611, is the last play Shakespeare wrote. (He may have collaborated on at least two other plays after *The Tempest*.) Many believe that Prospero's final speech in the play's epilogue is Shakespeare's own farewell speech as a playwright.

This play is one of Shakespeare's four romances (the other three are *Cymbeline, Pericles,* and *The Winter's Tale*). A major theme of romances is a restoration of losses. In *The Tempest*, Prospero regains his dukedom, and Alonso, the king, regains his son. Other themes include illusion versus reality, civilization versus nature, and power—the power of nature, the power of magic, the power to forgive, the power to enslave and set free, and dreams of power.

The Tempest is one of only a few of Shakespeare's plays that do not appear to have a single source. Shakespeare wrote the play at the time that the English were exploring the New World.

Shakespeare was aware of these explorations, and had heard tales of shipwrecks and stories about the natives; all of these probably contributed in some way to his writing of this play.

Activity: Divide students into small groups. Have each group write what they know about how Prospero left Milan and ended up on the island. Then, using these facts as a starting point, have each group write a mini-play detailing the events that led up to Prospero and Miranda leaving Milan and eventually landing on this island.

BARD CARD | **The Tempest**

Plot Summary: *The Tempest* is the story of a wise old magician who, with the help of the fates, regains his stolen dukedom and betroths his daughter to the Prince of Naples. This romance or tragicomedy takes place on an island in the 15th century.

Main Characters

Prospero: former and rightful Duke of Milan
Miranda: Prospero's daughter
Ferdinand: son of the King of Naples
Ariel: Prospero's spirit servant
Caliban: Prospero's slave
Alonso: King of Naples
Antonio: Prospero's brother, the wrongful Duke of Milan
Sebastian: Alonso's brother
Gonzalo: an honest man from Naples who saved Prospero and Miranda's lives
Trinculo: Alonso's jester
Stephano: Alonso's drunken butler

Glossary

allay: calm
auspicious: favorable
bellowing: shouting in a deep voice
boatswain: a naval officer
bondage: captivity
celestial: heavenly
charge: command
cherubim: angel child
din: a loud ongoing noise
elements: the four substances—air, water, fire, and earth—formerly believed to make up the physical universe

entreat: plead; beg
gales: winds
manacle: bind; shackle
piteous: compassionate
ratify: formally approve
supplant: replace by force or treachery
tempest: a violent storm
trod: walked
vexations: troubles
yare: set for action

Hamlet

by William Shakespeare

Hamlet might not have minded staying, for Ophelia—the woman he loved—was at Elsinore. But Ophelia's father, Polonius, told her not to return Hamlet's affection. Soon the prince heard some alarming news from his friend Horatio: He and two officers had seen the dead king's ghost stalking the battlements of the castle at midnight.

I WILL WATCH TO-NIGHT; PERCHANCE 'TWILL WALK AGAIN.

I WARRANT IT WILL.

After his father's sudden death, Hamlet, prince of Denmark, returned from the University of Wittenberg to Elsinore Castle. Hamlet's grief was compounded by his mother's hasty marriage to Claudius, the dead king's brother. Hamlet longed to return to Wittenberg to escape the sight of Claudius in his father's place. The king and queen wanted him to stay.

That night, Hamlet met Horatio and the officers on the guard platform. Shortly after midnight, the armed ghost of Hamlet's father appeared and beckoned to Hamlet to follow it. Horatio and the officers begged him not to go, but Hamlet followed the ghost.

The ghost led Hamlet to the battlements. There, the ghost told Hamlet that he had not died from the sting of a serpent, as people believed, but had been poisoned by Claudius, his brother and Hamlet's uncle.

MURDER! MY UNCLE!

AY, THE SERPENT THAT DID STING THY FATHER'S LIFE NOW WEARS HIS CROWN. IF THOU HAST NATURE IN THEE, BEAR IT NOT.

Rosencrantz and Guildenstern spoke to Hamlet. But the prince, guessing they were spies, told them nothing. When a group of actors arrived at the castle, Hamlet got an idea. He pulled aside one of the actors and quietly asked him to play *The Murder of Gonzago* the following night, with some minor changes.

YOU COULD STUDY A SPEECH WHICH I WOULD INSERT IN'T?

AY, MY LORD.

After this meeting with the ghost, Hamlet began to act crazy. Polonius thought it was because Ophelia rejected him; but the king was unsure. Was Hamlet really mad? Or was his craziness an act to gain the throne? The king sent for two young men to spy on Hamlet.

Hamlet planned for the actors to replay his father's murder so he could watch the king's reaction. But Hamlet still had his doubts. With his father's possible murder, his mother's disloyalty, and Ophelia's rejection, was life worth living?

At the play, Claudius stormed out during the scene where a man pours poison in his sleeping brother's ear. Convinced now that the ghost was telling the truth, Hamlet followed, ready to kill him. But he came upon the king praying. If Hamlet murdered Claudius then, the king would go straight to heaven.

UP, SWORD; AND KNOW THOU A MORE HORRID OCCASION FOR SEIZING.

Hearing of Polonius's death made the king even more fearful for his own life. He sent Hamlet to England with Rosencrantz and Guildenstern. The spies carried a letter from the king, the contents of which were known only to Claudius himself.

THE PRESENT DEATH OF HAMLET. DO IT, ENGLAND.

Later, Hamlet went to see his mother and began arguing with her. Upset, the queen cried out for help. Seeing the tapestry move, Hamlet drove his sword right through the fabric, thinking the king was behind it. But it wasn't the king; it was Polonius.

O, I AM SLAIN!

A BLOODY DEED! ALMOST AS BAD, GOOD MOTHER, AS KILL A KING, AND MARRY WITH HIS BROTHER.

O, WHAT A RASH AND BLOODY DEED THIS IS!

Laertes, son of Polonius, was in Paris when he heard of his father's death. He rushed home to Denmark, determined to avenge his father's murder. He became even more determined when he met his sister, Ophelia, and saw that their father's death had made her mad.

THEY BORE HIM BAREFACED ON THE BIER HEY NON NONNY, NONNY, HEY NONNY.

HADST THOU THY WITS, AND DIDST PERSUADE REVENGE, IT COULD NOT MOVE THUS.

eanwhile, Hamlet, unable to sleep on the ship, got up and stole the packet his companions were carrying. He discovered the orders for his death. Hamlet wrote new orders for Rosencrantz and Guildenstern's deaths, and resealed the packet. Then he escaped on a pirate ship headed for Denmark.

n case Laertes's poisoned sword tip did not work, the king also promised to poison Hamlet's drink at the match. As they were talking, the queen rushed in, crying that Ophelia was dead.

When Hamlet arrived in Denmark, he lied, saying he had been captured by pirates. The king trusted the prince even less now, and quickly planned to have Hamlet killed in a duel with Laertes. Laertes, eager to avenge his father's death, willingly went along with the plan.

I'LL ANOINT MY SWORD WITH SUCH POISON, THAT, IF I GALL HIM SLIGHTLY, IT MAY BE DEATH.

Hamlet, unaware of Ophelia's death, met Horatio in the churchyard. He told his friend how he discovered the king's secret orders to have him beheaded in England.

WHAT A KING IS THIS!

DOES IT NOT, THINK'ST THEE, STAND ME NOW UPON, TO QUIT HIM WITH THIS ARM?

amlet and Horatio watched a funeral procession approach. When Hamlet saw the king, queen, and Laertes, and heard Laertes grieving, he realized it was Ophelia who was being buried.

amlet and Laertes started dueling. While they fought, the king set out the poisoned cup for Hamlet. But instead the queen, his wife, drank from it. She fell at the same time that Hamlet and Laertes were both wounded by the same poisoned sword tip.

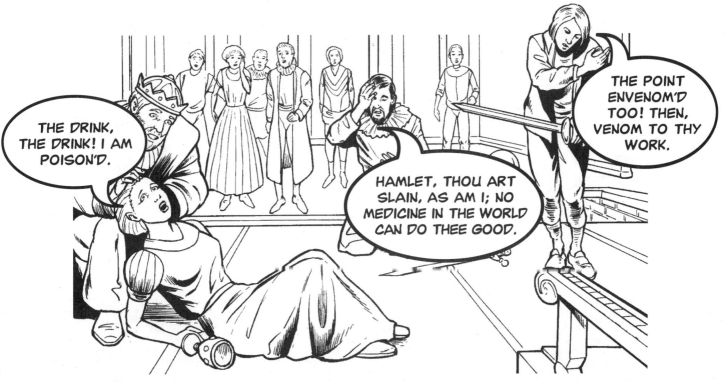

After the funeral, Hamlet accepted the king's invitation to a duel with Laertes. He told Horatio he believed he would win, yet he felt ill about his heart. This worried Horatio.

IF YOUR MIND DISLIKE ANY THING, OBEY IT.

NOT A WHIT. THE READINESS IS ALL: SINCE NO MAN HAS AUGHT OF WHAT HE LEAVES, WHAT IS'T TO LEAVE EARLY?

Hamlet stabbed the king with the poisoned sword. Claudius cried out and died. Then Laertes fell to the ground. Before he died, he and Hamlet forgave each other. Then Hamlet spoke his last words.

I AM DEAD, HORATIO. THOU LIVEST; REPORT ME AND MY CAUSE ARIGHT TO THE UNSATISFIED. TELL MY STORY.

Julius Caesar

by William Shakespeare

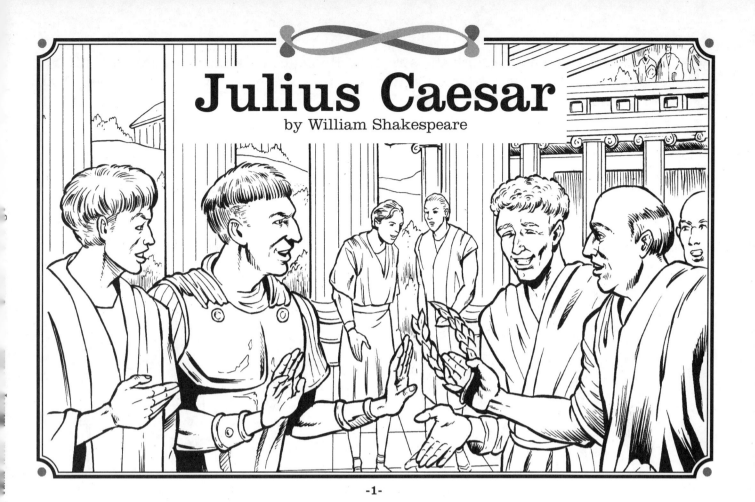

-1-

Caesar continued on his way, but Brutus stayed behind to speak with Caius Cassius. Cassius felt that Caesar was unworthy to rule. He hoped Brutus, one of Rome's most respected citizens, would agree with him. While the men spoke, they heard shouts in the distance.

WHAT MEANS THIS SHOUTING? I DO FEAR THE PEOPLE CHOOSE CAESAR FOR THEIR KING.

THEN MUST I THINK YOU WOULD NOT HAVE IT SO.

Julius Caesar paraded through the streets of Rome, celebrating yet another military victory. With him were his wife, Calpurnia, and his friends and fellow soldiers, Mark Antony and Marcus Brutus. The crowd pressed upon them, and one man called out to Caesar.

Neither heaven nor earth was at peace that night. Graves opened, fiery warriors fought upon the clouds, and a lioness whelped in the streets. Cassius, Casca, and Cinna met to plan how to overthrow Caesar, whom the senators intended to crown as king in the morning.

Brutus, at home, was disturbed over papers he found at his house. The papers urged him to "Speak, strike, and redress." Brutus thought the papers came from ordinary citizens. In fact, they were from Cassius, who wanted to convince Brutus that it was his duty to strike Caesar to save Rome.

The next day was the ides of March. Caesar's wife begged him not to leave the house, believing that the events of the night before were bad omens. She had also dreamed that his statue had one hundred holes, spouting blood. But Decius Brutus, whom Caesar wrongly believed to be his friend, arrived and convinced him otherwise.

When Cassius and the other conspirators arrived at Brutus's house, he readily agreed to join them. As the men planned Caesar's murder for the next morning, Cassius suggested they should kill Caesar's good friend, Mark Antony, as well. But Brutus refused.

Caesar walked the streets of Rome accompanied by Decius, Brutus, and others. Someone thrust a scroll at him that warned of the conspiracy, but Caesar did not read it. Then he saw the soothsayer and jeered at him.

Once in the Capitol, a conspirator took Mark Antony aside to get him out of the way. Then another conspirator approached Caesar with a petition. The others gathered around as if to second his petition. As Caesar refused it, they stabbed him 23 times.

Mark Antony returned to the Capitol. He assured Brutus that he was no enemy, and asked why they had thought Caesar was dangerous. Brutus said he would answer that question when he spoke at Caesar's funeral. Antony asked to be allowed to speak also. Brutus agreed.

Mark Antony, who fled at Caesar's murder, sent his servant back to the Capitol. He asked to return and speak to Brutus, to learn the reason for Caesar's death. Brutus sent the servant to tell his master that he should come to him, and that his safety was guaranteed.

Brutus told Antony to prepare the body and meet them at the Forum. After the conspirators left, Antony vowed to avenge Caesar's murder. A servant of Octavius Caesar, grandnephew of the dead ruler, arrived to say that his master, unaware of Caesar's death, was on his way to Rome.

Brutus spoke first at Caesar's funeral, saying that he rose against Caesar not because he loved Caesar less, but that he loved Rome more. Would the people rather have Caesar alive and they all die slaves, or have Caesar dead and they all live free men? The crowd cheered Brutus.

The people divided into two camps. One supported Mark Antony and Octavius Caesar; the other followed Brutus and Cassius. The latter had fled and set up camp in Sardis. Antony and Octavius gathered their forces and began marching toward them. The night before the two armies met on the plains of Philippi, Caesar's ghost visited Brutus.

Brutus asked the crowd to stay and listen to Antony, then left. Antony spoke of how Brutus said Caesar was ambitious, and reminded the people that Caesar had refused the crown. He said that Caesar loved them so much, that he had remembered every Roman citizen in his will.

Brutus and Cassius left Sardis for Philippi. They met Antony and Octavius on the battlefield before the fighting began.

The generals split up. Brutus fought against Octavius; Cassius against Antony. Brutus's forces were winning the battle against Caesar's nephew. Brutus sent Messala with orders for Cassius to come and help finish off this portion of the battle.

RIDE, RIDE, MESSALA, RIDE, AND GIVE THESE BILLS UNTO THE LEGIONS ON THE OTHER SIDE. LET THEM SET ON AT ONCE; FOR I PERCEIVE SUDDEN PUSH GIVES OCTAVIUS' WING THE OVERTHROW.

When Brutus learned of Cassius's death, his spirits fell, and the battle turned against him. Faced with defeat, Brutus ordered his servant Strato to hold his sword and turn his face away while Brutus fell upon it.

FAREWELL, GOOD STRATO. CAESAR, NOW BE STILL.

GIVE ME YOUR HAND FIRST. FARE YOU WELL, MY LORD.

On the other side of the battlefield, Cassius was losing to Antony. When he saw Messala and his men riding toward him, he thought they were foes, not friends. Believing all was lost, Cassius ordered his servant Pindarus to kill him.

GUIDE THOU THE SWORD. CAESAR, THOU ART REVENGED, EVEN WITH THE SWORD THAT KILLED THEE.

When Antony and Octavius reached where Brutus had stood, they found him dead.

THIS WAS THE NOBLEST ROMAN OF THEM ALL: ALL THE CONSPIRATORS SAVE ONLY HE DID THAT THEY DID IN ENVY OF GREAT CAESAR; HE ONLY, IN A GENERAL HONEST THOUGHT AND COMMON GOOD TO ALL, MADE ONE OF THEM.

King Lear

by William Shakespeare

The king asked Cordelia to mend her speech a little, but Cordelia would give him nothing more than a simple expression of love. Angered, Lear told her that she was no longer his daughter. The Earl of Kent stepped in and asked the king to reconsider.

King Lear of Britain planned to divide his kingdom equally among his three daughters. Before doing so, he asked them to declare publicly how much they loved him. Goneril and Regan swore that they loved their father better than anything in the world. Then Lear turned to his youngest—and favorite—daughter, Cordelia.

NOW, OUR JOY, ALTHOUGH THE LAST, NOT LEAST, SPEAK.

I CANNOT HEAVE MY HEART INTO MY MOUTH: I LOVE YOUR MAJESTY ACCORDING TO MY BOND.

Kent continued arguing, and Lear banished him. Then the ruler told the two men who had wanted to marry Cordelia that her only dowry would be his curse. The Duke of Burgundy refused her hand. But the King of France did not care and took her as his queen.

LET HER BE THINE; FOR WE HAVE NO SUCH DAUGHTER.

FAIREST CORDELIA, THEE AND THY VIRTUES HERE I SEIZE UPON.

After dividing his kingdom between Goneril and Regan, Lear went to stay with Goneril and her husband, the Duke of Albany. Goneril did not like having all of Lear's followers around. She demanded that her father get rid of half of them. He refused, and vowed to stay with Regan instead.

HOW SHARPER THAN A SERPENT'S TOOTH IT IS TO HAVE A THANKLESS CHILD! AWAY, AWAY!

Oswald's cries brought Regan, Cornwall, and Gloucester. Regan and Cornwall put Kent into stocks for being disrespectful. Gloucester asked them not to treat the king's servant this way, but they refused to listen. When Lear arrived a short while later, he asked his servant who put him in stocks.

YOUR SON AND DAUGHTER.

THEY COULD NOT, WOULD NOT DO'T.

Kent had disguised himself as a servant so Lear wouldn't recognize him. Lear sent Kent ahead with a letter to Regan. Goneril also sent her steward, Oswald, to deliver a letter to Regan. Kent and Oswald met at the Earl of Gloucester's castle, where Regan and her husband, the Duke of Cornwall, were staying.

The king called for Regan and Cornwall. He told Regan how Goneril had abused him. Regan answered, saying that Goneril did nothing wrong, and that Lear should ask for her forgiveness. Lear did not want to return to Goneril.

Lear reminded Regan that he had given her half of his kingdom, but she refused to be moved. When Goneril arrived, the two sisters made fun of their father until Lear left them, mad with grief. A storm came up, and Gloucester wanted to go after the king.

When Kent found Lear, he was ranting to his Fool on the stormy heath. Kent found a hovel where his master could take shelter from the storm. The king sent Kent and his Fool in first, then, reluctantly, followed.

Kent was released from the stocks and went after his master. On the way, he learned from a gentleman that the army of France was in Dover, preparing to attack England. He sent this gentleman to find Cordelia, and tell her of her sisters' abuse of their father.

Meanwhile, Gloucester received a letter informing him that the French army had landed at Dover to avenge the king's injuries. He shared the news with his son Edmund, asking him to keep it secret, while he looked for the king.

loucester found King Lear, his Fool, and Kent in a hut on the heath. The king seemed mad, so Gloucester warned Kent, whom he did not recognize, to get Lear to safety for his daughters sought his death. He led them to a farmhouse near the castle where they were to wait for a carriage that would bring them to Dover.

ornwall sent Goneril to inform her husband that the French army had landed. Then he and Regan turned to Gloucester, who had just been caught. They bound him, and Cornwall questioned him. When Gloucester refused to cooperate, Cornwall put his eyes out.

While Gloucester helped his king, Edmund betrayed his father. He took Gloucester's secret of the French invasion to the Duke of Cornwall. Regan's husband declared Edmund's father a traitor, and named Edmund the new Earl of Gloucester.

SEEK OUT WHERE THY FATHER IS, THAT HE MAY BE READY FOR OUR APPREHENSION.

When Goneril returned to Albany, he was appalled to learn that Edmund had also turned against his father. He called his wife a devil. She called him a coward. Then a messenger came with the news that Cornwall was dead, killed by a servant as he put out Gloucester's eyes.

GLOUCESTER, I LIVE TO THANK THEE FOR THE LOVE THOU SHOWED'ST THE KING, AND TO REVENGE THINE EYES.

Thanks to Gloucester's foresight and Kent's guidance, King Lear was soon safe in Dover. Lear was truly like a madman then, dressed with wild flowers. When he first saw Cordelia, he did not recognize her. When he realized who she was, he fell to his knees in repentance.

PRAY YOU NOW, FORGET AND FORGIVE: I AM OLD AND FOOLISH.

O, LOOK UPON ME, SIR. YOU MUST NOT KNEEL.

Before Albany could find out where Edmund had sent Lear and Cordelia, Edmund's honest brother, Edgar, appeared. He called Edmund a traitor, and the two fought. Mortally wounded, Edmund confessed that he had ordered Cordelia to be hanged.

QUICKLY, SEND A MESSENGER TO THE CASTLE, FOR MY WRIT IS ON THE LIFE OF CORDELIA.

RUN, RUN, O, RUN! THE GODS DEFEND HER!

he British armies had soon set up camp near Dover. Despite his misgivings, Albany felt he had to defend British soil against a foreign invader, and joined Edmund at the camp. They weren't there long when Edmund captured King Lear and Cordelia.

ut it was too late. Within minutes, Lear appeared carrying his dead daughter, whom he had tried but failed to save. He was followed by his faithful friend Kent, whom he had finally recognized. When the king reached Albany and Edgar, he fell to the ground.

Macbeth

by William Shakespeare

The witches also told Banquo that he would be the father of kings. Macbeth, who was already Thane of Glamis, asked the witches why they called him Thane of Cawdor and king; but they vanished without answering. Just then, two of the king's men appeared.

THE KING BADE US GIVE THIS HONOR.

THAT HE SHALL CALL MACBETH THANE OF CAWDOR.

CAN THE DEVIL SPEAK TRUE?

GLAMIS, AND THANE OF CAWDOR! HAPPY PROLOGUES OF THE IMPERIAL THEME.

Macbeth and his friend Banquo were returning victorious from a battle against Vikings and Scottish rebels. As the two Scottish noblemen crossed a lonely heath, they came upon three witches.

Macbeth wrote to his wife of the witches' prophecies. Lady Macbeth read the letter with great excitement. When a messenger told her that Macbeth was on his way home, and that King Duncan was with him, the witches' final prophecy seemed close to fulfillment.

Macbeth's conscience troubled him. Duncan was his kinsman and his king, as well as his guest. Lady Macbeth reminded her husband of the "ornament of life" he so desired. Macbeth and his wife plotted to murder Duncan in his sleep.

The next morning, the noble Macduff went to wake the king and found him murdered. He cried out in horror. Macbeth rushed into the king's chambers and killed the groomsmen, who appeared guilty of the murder. Banquo and Lady Macbeth hurried to the king's bedchamber.

That night, Macbeth stole into the king's bedchamber and stabbed Duncan in the heart. He returned to his wife, bloody daggers in hand, horrified at what he had done. Lady Macbeth hurried back to smear the king's sleeping grooms with the bloody daggers before dropping them on their pillows. Then she returned to her chamber.

WILL ALL GREAT NEPTUNE'S OCEAN WASH THIS BLOOD CLEAN FROM MY HAND?

A LITTLE WATER CLEARS US OF THIS DEED.

When Duncan's two sons learned of their father's death, they feared for their own lives. Malcolm fled to England, Donalbain to Ireland. That left Macbeth as Duncan's closest kinsman and heir to the throne. Macbeth and his wife quickly set off to Scone where Macbeth was crowned King.

Macbeth did not settle easily at the king's palace, for there was one whom he greatly feared and envied: Banquo.

Shortly after the feast began, the murderers reported that they had slit Banquo's throat, but his son had managed to escape. Macbeth sent them off and returned to the feast. To his horror, Banquo's ghost was sitting on his stool!

anquo's talk worried Macbeth, but the witches' prophecy that Banquo's heirs would be kings worried him even more. He invited Banquo and his son to a feast, then arranged to have them murdered on their way to the celebration.

rightened by Banquo's ghost, and haunted by the thought of Banquo's son succeeding him, Macbeth worried about his future as king. He searched for the witches to hear what the future would bring.

When Macbeth left the witches' cavern, he learned that Macduff had fled to England to help Malcolm raise an army to avenge his father's death and take the crown from Macbeth. Macbeth ordered an army to the home of Macduff, Thane of Fife.

The murder of Lady Macduff and her entire family proved too much for Lady Macbeth to bear. She began to walk and talk in her sleep. A doctor was brought in to see if he could help her.

Macduff and Malcolm were preparing an army to return to Scotland when Macduff learned that Macbeth had brutally murdered his entire family.

When a messenger brought news to Macbeth that an army of ten thousand English troops was advancing on the castle at Dunsinane, the king called for his armor. Remembering the witches' recent prophecies gave him courage.

Malcolm's army was passing through Birnam Wood when the leader had an idea. He ordered every soldier to cut down a bough and carry it before him, to hide the army's numbers.

On the battlefield, Macbeth remembered the witches' prophecy that no man of woman born could harm him. He fought fearlessly. Then he met Macduff, the man the witches warned him about. Still, he did not fear.

Inside Dunsinane, Macbeth was grieving at the news that his wife was killed by her own sorrow. Then a messenger arrived with more bad news: While on lookout, he saw Birnam Wood began to move!

So the witches' prophecy was fulfilled once again. With a flourish of his sword, Macduff cut off Macbeth's head. Then he carried the traitor's head to Malcolm and laid it at his feet.

A Midsummer Night's Dream

by William Shakespeare

A father's word was law in Athens. Theseus warned Hermia that if she disobeyed her father, she would be placed in a nunnery or put to death. Hermia announced she would rather become a nun than marry Demetrius, when she loved Lysander. The duke gave her a few days to think about her future.

heseus, Duke of Athens, was to marry Hippolyta, Queen of the Amazons, in four days. While they were discussing their wedding, a very upset Egeus interrupted them. With him were his daughter, Hermia, and the two men who loved her, Demetrius and Lysander.

MY GOOD EGEUS: WHAT'S THE NEWS WITH THEE?

FULL OF VEXATION COME I, WITH COMPLAINT AGAINST MY CHILD, MY DAUGHTER HERMIA. DEMETRIUS HATH MY CONSENT TO MARRY HER YET LYSANDER HATH BEWITCH'D THE BOSOM OF MY CHILD.

ysander reminded the duke that Demetrius had previously wooed Helena. The duke took Demetrius and Egeus away to speak with them. Hippolyta followed. Left alone, Hermia and Lysander made plans to meet in the forest the next night and run away. As they spoke, Helena arrived, lamenting Demetrius's love of Hermia.

TAKE COMFORT: HE NO MORE SHALL SEE MY FACE.

TO-MORROW NIGHT, THROUGH ATHENS' GATES WE STEAL.

I WILL GO TELL HIM OF FAIR HERMIA'S FLIGHT: IF I HAVE THANKS IT IS A DEAR EXPENSE.

Meanwhile, a group of Athenian craftsmen had heard that the duke was looking for entertainment for his wedding. They hoped to perform a play one of them had written, called *The Most Lamentable Comedy, and Most Cruel Death of Pyramus and Thisby.* They met to choose parts.

HERE ARE YOUR PARTS. MEMORIZE THEM BY TO-MORROW NIGHT; AND MEET ME IN THE PALACE WOOD A MILE, WITHOUT THE TOWN.

THERE WE MAY REHEARSE MOST COURAGEOUSLY.

Angry Oberon asked Robin Goodfellow to fetch the purple flower once struck by Cupid's arrow. The flower's juice, when placed on sleeping eyelids, made the victim fall in love with the first creature it sees. He planned to place it on Titania's eyes to embarrass her by making her fall in love with an animal.

AND ERE I TAKE THIS CHARM FROM OFF HER SIGHT I'LL MAKE HER RENDER UP HER PAGE TO ME.

The woods were more than a place for lovers to meet and craftsmen to rehearse. There, fairies also held their revels. Though that night, there was more arguing than revelry. The king of the fairies was angry because the queen would not give him her page.

As Robin fetched the flower, Oberon spied Helena chasing Demetrius, who was searching for Hermia in the woods. Helena told Demetrius she loved him, but Demetrius declared he could never return her love. When Robin returned with the flower, Oberon anointed Titania's eyes, then asked Robin to cast a spell, too.

ermia and Lysander were also in the woods, running away as planned. Tired from their travels, they laid down on a grassy bank and fell asleep. Robin came upon the two lovers, saw Lysander's Athenian garments, and mistakenly anointed his eyes with the bewitching juice.

elena ran off and Lysander chased after her. Then Hermia awoke, crying out for Lysander. She had dreamed a serpent ate her heart, while Lysander watched and smiled. When Lysander did not answer, Hermia became increasingly upset.

Robin left the sleeping couple. Then Helena, lost after Demetrius abandoned her in the dark woods, stumbled upon Lysander, waking him. Lysander instantly fell in love with Helena, saying it was her, not Hermia, whom he loved. Helena thought that he was mocking her.

-10-

In another part of the forest, Robin Goodfellow came upon the tradesmen's rehearsal. When the puck realized the fairy queen slept nearby, he slipped an ass's head on the shoulders of Nick Bottom. The other tradesmen ran away in fear. Bottom, unaware of his transformation, thought they were teasing him.

-12-

Bottom's singing woke the fairy queen. When she opened her eyes, which Oberon had anointed with the flower's juice, the first thing she saw was Bottom's hairy head. Titania instantly fell in love.

When Oberon saw that Demetrius was still in love with Hermia, he realized Robin's mistake. After Hermia ran off in search of Lysander, and Demetrius laid down to rest, Oberon sent Robin to find and bring back Helena. Then he himself anointed Demetrius's eyes with the purple flower's juice.

obin returned to Oberon and reported that Titania had fallen in love with a fool wearing an ass's head. Oberon was delighted with the news. Robin also said that he had anointed the Athenian's eyes. As they spoke, Oberon and Robin spied Demetrius and Hermia arguing nearby.

obin led Helena, who was being pursued by Lysander, back to where Demetrius was sleeping. The sound of their voices woke Demetrius. He opened his eyes, looked at Helena, and fell madly in love with her—much to Helena's surprise and disbelief.

While Demetrius and Lysander declared their love to Helena, Hermia appeared. Her happiness at finding Lysander quickly faded when he told her that he no longer loved her—it was Helena he now loved. Oberon ordered Robin to put the men to sleep and remove the charm on Lysander's eyes.

As the king and queen danced in one part of the forest, the four young lovers slept in another. They were soon wakened when Theseus and Hippolyta came upon them while hunting. Demetrius immediately pledged his love to Helena, and Lysander to Hermia.

While Robin took care of the young lovers, Oberon went to visit Titania. She was so captivated with Bottom that she willingly gave Oberon the page he had wanted. Later, as the queen and Bottom slept in each other's arms, Oberon removed the spell from Titania. Robin looked on as Oberon woke his queen.

The three couples were married that evening. Theseus chose the tradesmen's play for entertainment. Afterwards, the newlyweds retired to their chambers. As everyone fell asleep, Oberon, Titania, and their train of fairies danced through the palace.

Much Ado About Nothing

by William Shakespeare

While Leonato introduced his daughter, Hero, to Don Pedro and Claudio, Benedick and Leonato's niece, Beatrice, spoke. From their tone, it was clear that they already knew each other. It was also clear that there was no love lost between them.

Don Pedro, Prince of Arragon, came to Messina to visit Leonato, the governor, on his way home from a battle against his half-brother, Don John. With him came his friends, the young lords Claudio and Benedick, as well as Don John, with whom he had reconciled. Leonato warmly welcomed Don Pedro.

After their hosts had left to prepare a feast for them, Claudio confided to Benedick that he had fallen in love with the governor's daughter. Benedick was appalled. Don Pedro laughed to hear Benedick swear he would never marry.

That night there was a masked ball. Beatrice spoke to a masked man whom she didn't realize was Benedick. The words she used to describe him stung the prince's friend.

Don Pedro then asked for and received Leonato's approval of the marriage of Claudio and Hero. The prince and governor called the young couple and told them the good news. They were overjoyed.

At the ball, a masked Don Pedro wooed Hero for Claudio. Then the prince spoke with Beatrice. Taken by her beauty and wit, he half-heartedly proposed to her. She refused, for she thought little of marriage as well. Don Pedro later told Leonato about his niece's refusal.

SHE CANNOT HEAR TELL OF A HUSBAND.

SHE WERE AN EXCELLENT WIFE FOR BENEDICK.

Then the prince proposed a plan to help the week pass quickly: He would use the time to make Benedick and Beatrice fall in love with each other. He asked if the others would help him fashion this plan.

MY LORD, I AM FOR YOU.

I WILL DO ANY MODEST OFFICE, MY LORD, TO HELP MY COUSIN TO A GOOD HUSBAND.

AND I, MY LORD.

While Don Pedro planned to bring Benedick and Beatrice together, his half-brother plotted to keep Claudio and Hero apart. Bitter over how Claudio had beaten him in battle, Don John and his follower, Borachio, planned to trick Claudio into believing that Hero loved Borachio, not Claudio.

MY CUNNING SHALL NOT SHAME ME.

BE CUNNING IN THE WORKING THIS, AND THY FEE IS A THOUSAND DUCATS.

After Don Pedro and the other men tricked Benedick, Hero and her waiting woman prepared to trick Beatrice. They, too, took a walk in the orchard, and spoke when they knew Beatrice was nearby.

CAN THIS BE TRUE? BENEDICK, LOVE ON; I WILL REQUITE THEE.

BUT ARE YOU SURE THAT BENEDICK LOVES BEATRICE SO ENTIRELY?

SO SAYS THE PRINCE AND MY NEW-TROTHED LORD.

Don Pedro put his plan into action. He, Claudio, and Leonato walked in the orchard near where Benedick was reading, knowing he could overhear them. Don Pedro asked Leonato if it was true that his niece Beatrice loved Benedick.

SHE DOTH INDEED; MY DAUGHTER SAYS SO.

SHE SAYS BEATRICE WILL DIE IF HE LOVE HER NOT, AND SHE WILL DIE ERE SHE MAKE HER LOVE KNOWN.

WHEN I SAID I WOULD DIE A BACHELOR, I DID NOT THINK I SHOULD LIVE TILL I WERE MARRIED.

The night before the wedding, Don Pedro, Claudio, and Leonato teased Benedick, saying he looked lovesick. He admitted that this was true, and asked to speak to Leonato alone. After they left, Don John arrived and told the prince and Claudio that Hero was disloyal.

MAY THIS BE SO?

I WILL NOT THINK IT.

IF YOU WILL FOLLOW ME, I WILL SHOW YOU ENOUGH.

on John led Don Pedro and Claudio to Hero's window. There they saw Borachio embracing a woman and calling her Hero. The prince and his friend were outraged.

eatrice, accompanying Hero to her wedding, confessed that she was in love. At the church, they met Friar Francis, Leonato, Benedick, Don Pedro, Claudio, and Don John. When the friar asked if anyone knew any reason Hero and Claudio should not be married, Claudio spoke up.

Later, the night watchmen overheard Borachio bragging that Don John had paid him a thousand gold coins for deceiving the prince and Claudio. The watch arrested Borachio. The next morning, the constables stopped Leonato on his way to his daughter's wedding.

WE WOULD HAVE HIM EXAMINED BEFORE YOUR LORDSHIP.

SIR, OUR WATCH TO-NIGHT HAVE TA'EN AS ARRANT A KNAVE AS ANY.

TAKE THE EXAMINATION YOURSELF AND BRING IT ME: I AM NOW IN GREAT HASTE.

Denying the accusation, Hero collapsed. Claudio, Don Pedro, and Don John left the church. Leonato said he hoped his daughter was dead, as it would be "the fairest cover for her shame." The friar, who believed that Hero was innocent, suggested that they pretend that she was indeed dead while they searched for the truth.

COME, LADY, DIE TO LIVE: THIS WEDDING-DAY PERHAPS IS BUT PROLONG'D.

Everyone left the church, save Beatrice and Benedick. Beatrice wept over how Hero had been treated, and Benedick tried to comfort her. He said that he also believed her cousin had been wronged. Then, for the first time, the two professed their love to each other.

The next morning, Claudio and Don Pedro met the friar, Leonato, and Benedick at the church. As Claudio stepped up to the altar, one of several masked women stepped forward as well. The friar performed the marriage ceremony. Then Claudio lifted his wife's mask. It was Hero.

Leonato's shame and anger dissolved when he heard Borachio's confession: Don John had arranged the awful deception. When Don Pedro and Claudio learned the truth, they felt they had killed Hero. The governor told Claudio he could clear his daughter's name, visit her tomb, then marry his niece.

Benedick then asked for Beatrice. She stepped forward and took off her mask. When he asked if she loved him, she answered no more than reason. He said the same. Then Hero and Claudio revealed sonnets that Benedick and Beatrice had written for each other.

Romeo & Juliet

by William Shakespeare

One of old Capulet's servants approached Romeo and Benvolio. Unaware that they were Montagues, the servant asked them to help him read the names of people whom Capulet wanted to invite to a party that night. After the servant left, Benvolio got an idea.

Romeo, the only son of old Montague, walked the streets of Verona, Italy, unaware that the prince had just broken up yet another fight between his family and the Capulets. Romeo's mind was not on the ancient family feud, but on Rosaline, a girl who did not return his love. Benvolio tried to cheer up his friend.

Romeo, Benvolio, and Romeo's best friend, Mercutio, stood outside Capulet's house before the party. They wore masks to hide their faces. Romeo wondered if it was a good idea to go into his family's enemy's house like this.

The first person Romeo noticed at the party was Capulet's beautiful daughter, Juliet. He did not know who she was, only that "he ne'er saw true beauty till this night." When Tybalt, Juliet's cousin, heard Romeo, he recognized a Montague's voice. He wanted to fight Romeo, but old Capulet stopped him.

I WILL WITHDRAW: BUT THIS INTRUSION SHALL NOW SEEMING SWEET, CONVERT TO BITTER GALL.

CONTENT THEE, GENTLE COZ, LET HIM ALONE. I WOULD NOT FOR THE WEALTH OF ALL THE TOWN HERE IN MY HOUSE DO HIM DISPARAGEMENT.

Later, Juliet asked the nurse who the man was with whom she had been speaking. Her nurse did not know, and went to ask someone. When she returned, she told Juliet that his name was Romeo, and that he was a Montague, "the only son of your great enemy."

MY ONLY LOVE SPRUNG FROM MY ONLY HATE! TOO EARLY SEEN UNKNOWN, AND KNOWN TOO LATE!

omeo approached Juliet and they spoke. Romeo kissed her hand, then her lips. They were together only a few moments when the nurse came and told Juliet that her mother wanted to speak with her. As Juliet walked away, Romeo asked the nurse who Juliet was. She told him that she was Capulet's only daughter.

IS SHE A CAPULET? O DEAR ACCOUNT! MY LIFE IS MY FOE'S DEBT.

omeo left the party, but could not go home when his heart was filled with Juliet. He turned back and leapt over an orchard wall to be near where she lived. Moments later, Juliet appeared on the balcony. Unaware that Romeo stood below in her garden, she began speaking.

O ROMEO, ROMEO! WHEREFORE ART THOU ROMEO? ROMEO, DOFF THY NAME, AND FOR THY NAME WHICH IS NO PART OF THEE TAKE ALL MYSELF.

omeo stepped from the shadows and answered Juliet's vows of love with his own. Juliet told Romeo that if his purpose was marriage, to send word to her tomorrow, and she would come to him. Then the nurse called for Juliet to come inside.

uliet left the monastery and went home to wait for Romeo that night. On his way home, Romeo came upon Mercutio and Benvolio arguing with Tybalt. The young Capulet, still angry about the previous night, called Romeo a villain. Romeo, remembering that Tybalt was Juliet's cousin, refused to return the insult.

Romeo went to speak to Friar Laurence. He agreed to marry them, hoping that their union would end the ancient family feud. Romeo sent word to Juliet, and she met him at the monastery the following afternoon. There they were secretly married.

Mercutio, angry at Tybalt's insult, drew his sword and challenged the young Capulet. Tybalt quickly drew his sword and killed Mercutio. In anger and grief over his best friend's death, Romeo forgot his efforts at peacemaking, drew his sword, and killed Tybalt.

When Juliet learned that Tybalt was dead and that the prince had banished Romeo for her cousin's murder, she was overcome with grief. Tybalt's death was woe enough, but Romeo's banishment was like "father, mother, Tybalt, Romeo, Juliet, all slain, all dead."

-13-

Romeo went to Juliet. Before dawn, he fled for Mantua. When Juliet's mother and father found her crying, they thought she was grieving over her cousin's death. They arranged for her immediate marriage to the young nobleman Paris. When Juliet said she could not marry him, her parents threatened to disown her.

-15-

Romeo hid in the abbey, desperate at the thought of being banished and never seeing Juliet again. The nurse arrived and told him that Juliet needed to see him. Friar Laurence advised Romeo to go to her, but to leave Verona before daybreak. He told him to hide in Mantua, where he would send word when it was safe to return.

Juliet ran to Friar Laurence for help, declaring she would kill herself before she would marry Paris. That gave the friar an idea. He told Juliet to agree to be married. On the night before the wedding, she should drink a potion that would put her in a death sleep for 42 hours. She would be laid to rest in the family tomb. The friar would make sure Romeo was by her side when she awoke.

Juliet went home and asked her parents for forgiveness. She then agreed to marry Paris the next day. That night, Juliet drank the friar's potion. When the nurse went to wake Juliet the next morning, she found her seemingly dead. The nurse's cries brought Lady Capulet and her husband.

Romeo found Juliet lying cold in the tomb. He drank the poison, gave her one last kiss, and died. Upon waking, Juliet found Romeo by her side, dead. She saw the empty poison cup. Then her eyes fell on Romeo's dagger. She picked it up and pointed it towards her chest.

Friar Laurence had written Romeo of the secret plan, asking him to hurry back to Verona. But the letter never reached him. When Romeo heard of Juliet's death, he bought a dram of poison. On horseback, he hurried back to Verona to the vault where Juliet lay.

When Romeo and Juliet were found dead, the friar told all what had happened. The prince scolded Capulet and Montague, saying their hate had caused heaven "to kill your joys with love." The two former enemies made peace and promised to erect golden statues of each other's child. Then the prince closed the vault.

The Tempest

by William Shakespeare

A lovely young woman and her father watched the shipwreck from an island in this tempestuous sea. The young woman, Miranda, begged her father, Prospero, to calm the storm.

TELL YOUR PITEOUS HEART THERE'S NO HARM DONE. I HAVE DONE NOTHING BUT IN CARE OF THEE.

IF BY YOUR ART, MY DEAREST FATHER, YOU HAVE PUT THE WILD WATERS IN THIS ROAR, ALLAY THEM.

Alonso, the King of Naples, was sailing home from his daughter's wedding to the King of Tunis. With him were his son Ferdinand, Antonio, the Duke of Milan, and other members of his court. On the Mediterranean Sea, they sailed into a terrible storm. The vessel was dashed to pieces, and all aboard were forced to abandon ship.

Then the magician told his daughter that before they came to the island twelve years earlier, he had been Duke of Milan. While he studied magic, his brother, Antonio, plotted his overthrow. One night, with the help of the King of Naples, Antonio set Prospero and three-year-old Miranda adrift in a small boat in the open sea.

Prospero explained that they would not have survived if not for his noble friend, Gonzalo. He secretly supplied the boat with food, water, and Prospero's much-loved magic books. These helped them get by until they reached land.

AND NOW, I PRAY YOU, SIR, YOUR REASON FOR RAISING THIS SEA-STORM?

BY ACCIDENT MOST STRANGE, BOUNTIFUL FORTUNE, HATH MINE ENEMIES BROUGHT TO THIS SHORE.

Prospero told Ariel to use his magic to lure the king's son to Miranda. Then Prospero called his other servant, Caliban. The grotesque creature reluctantly appeared, complaining that the island belonged to him, not Prospero. It had once belonged to his mother. Prospero called Caliban an untrainable savage.

HAG-SEED, HENCE! FETCH US IN FUEL; AND BE QUICK.

I MUST OBEY: HIS ART IS OF SUCH POWER.

Prospero summoned his servant Ariel, a magical spirit, who reported that all of the ship's passengers and crew were safe on different parts of the island. Ferdinand, the king's son, was alone on one corner. The king, Antonio, the king's brother, and Gonzalo were on another part. Two crew members wandered the island, while the rest slept on the ship, which was hidden in the harbor.

-6-

Ariel, turned invisible, found Ferdinand mourning for his father, whom he believed was lost at sea. Singing a song, Ariel led the king's son to Miranda, who was standing by her father's side. The two young people fell in love instantly. Prospero intervened.

-8-

On another part of the island, King Alonso mourned the loss of his son, whom he believed drowned. When the king and Gonzalo fell asleep, Antonio plotted with Sebastian, the king's brother, to kill the other two so that Sebastian could become king. As the traitorous brothers drew their swords, the invisible Ariel woke Gonzalo.

WHY ARE YOUR SWORDS DRAWN? WHAT'S THE MATTER?

GOOD ANGELS PRESERVE THE KING.

WE HEARD A BURST OF BELLOWING LIKE BULLS.

O, 'TWAS A DIN TO FRIGHT A MONSTER'S EAR!

-9-

Prospero had put Ferdinand to work rolling logs to test the prince's love for his daughter. Miranda disobeyed her father and visited the prisoner. She did not know that Prospero was watching from a distance as the two lovers exchanged vows.

I AM YOUR WIFE, IF YOU WILL MARRY ME.

AY, WITH A HEART AS WILLING AS BONDAGE E'ER OF FREEDOM: HERE'S MY HAND.

-11-

Meanwhile, Caliban was getting wood for Prospero when he met Trinculo, Alonso's jester, and Stephano, the king's drunken butler. At first he was afraid of these men, but his feelings changed after Stephano gave him some of his liquor to drink.

Ariel continued to fly around the island, checking on his charges. When he came upon Caliban, Stephano, and Trinculo, he heard the drunken trio plotting to kill Prospero.

On the other side of the island, King Alonso and his men were searching in vain for Ferdinand. Exhausted, they sat down to rest. When they did so, they began to hear wonderful music. Then a table appeared before them, laden with a lavish banquet.

WILL'T PLEASE YOU TASTE OF WHAT IS HERE?

I WILL STAND TO AND FEED, ALTHOUGH MY LAST: NO MATTER, SINCE I FEEL THE BEST IS PAST.

Meanwhile, Prospero went to see Miranda and Ferdinand. He told Ferdinand that all his vexations were but trials of his love, and that he had passed the test. He gave the young couple his blessings, then sent them inside his home to rest.

O, FERDINAND, HERE, AFORE HEAVEN, I RATIFY THIS MY RICH GIFT, MY DAUGHTER.

All the men rose to dine, but as they did so, thunder and lightning shook the air. Ariel flew down and clapped his wings on the table, making the banquet vanish. Then he turned and addressed King Alonso, Sebastian, and Duke Antonio.

YOU ARE THREE MEN OF SIN. FROM MILAN DID YOU SUPPLANT GOOD PROSPERO; UNTO THE SEA, HIM AND HIS INNOCENT CHILD.

O, THE NAME OF PROSPER. THE THUNDER PROCLAIMED MY SIN. THEREFORE MY SON I'THE OOZE IS BEDDED.

Hearing of Caliban's plot, Prospero instructed Ariel to hang fancy clothes on the tree in front of his house. When Caliban, Stephano, and Trinculo arrived to murder Prospero, the two shipmates were so distracted by the finery that they forgot why they came. Caliban tried to remind them, but they wouldn't listen. Then, Prospero and Ariel sent spirits in the shape of dogs to chase them away.

LET THEM BE HUNTED SOUNDLY. AT THIS HOUR LIE AT MY MERCY ALL MINE ENEMIES.

riel then told Prospero that his enemies seemed truly sorry for what they had done to him. Hearing that, the wise old man vowed to take part "with my nobler reason 'gainst my fury." He told Ariel to bring the king and his men to him.

There was further reason to rejoice when Ariel came forward with the master of the ship and the boatswain. Happy to find their king alive, they reported on the condition of their ship, which they so recently declared split.

Prospero embraced his friend, Gonzalo. He forgave Antonio, but demanded that he give back his dukedom. Then, hearing the king speak about the loss of his son, he led Alonso into his house, where Ferdinand and Miranda were playing chess. Father and son were overjoyed to see each other.

THOUGH THE SEAS THREATEN, THEY ARE MERCIFUL.

IF THIS PROVE A VISION OF THE ISLAND, ONE DEAR SON SHALL I TWICE LOSE.

Prospero told the king that he would explain all the strange events that had occurred. He said they would set sail for Naples in the morning, where Miranda and Ferdinand would be married. Then Prospero would return to Milan, to his dukedom. Before going inside, Prospero called for Ariel.

MY CHICK, ARIEL, CALM SEAS AND AUSPICIOUS GALES, THAT IS THY CHARGE. THEN TO THE ELEMENTS BE FREE, AND FARE THOU WELL!